These adventures
belong to:

....

....

....

....

....

First published in the United Kingdom in 2016 by Nosy Crow Ltd
The Crow's Nest, 10a Lant Street
London SE1 1QR
www.nosycrow.com

ISBN 978 0 85763 618 8

The 50 THINGS TO DO BEFORE YOU'RE 11¾ campaign was designed
for the National Trust by 18 Feet & Rising. Based on original concept and
content by Behaviour Change with design work by N. Duncan Mills.

A CIP catalogue record for this book is available from the British Library.

Printed in China by Imago

Papers used by Nosy Crow are made from wood grown in sustainable
forests.

10 9 8 7 6 5 4 3 2

50

THINGS TO DO
BEFORE YOU'RE

11 $\frac{3}{4}$

nosy crow

CONTENTS

RANGER

EXPLORER

TRACKER

YOU DID IT

ACTIVITIES

50 things to do before you're 11 ¾

Welcome to the great outdoors . . .

In this book, there's everything you need to have an excellent adventure! With help from kids all over the country, we've put together a list of great challenges; the ultimate 50 things to do before you're 11 ¾. Are you ready? Let's get exploring!

Who's it for?

Whether you're creative and crafty or you're an active explorer, this book is packed with activities that are fun for everyone! You can do them on your own, with your friends, or with your family. And you don't have to be under 11 ¾ – so don't leave the grown-ups behind!

Let's go!

You can do these activities almost anywhere you want – in your back garden, your local park or at a nearby National Trust place. To find somewhere near you, check out the 50 things app or visit: 50things.org.uk

Note to grown-ups

We recommend that you use your own judgement about what is safe and suitable for your children, and supervise these activities where necessary. If your little explorers are handling animals, don't forget to put them back where they came from.

Meet the gang

First things first, there are a few people we'd like you to meet. Say hello to Craig, Rae and Mia . . .

CRAIG

Age: 7½
Likes: Running, climbing, playing . . . anything outdoors!
Dislikes: Spiders
Favourite activity: Roll down a really big hill
Explorer type: Active explorer

Map – check!
Compass – check!
Water bottle – check!
That's everything!

These guys have all the know-how you need to complete your 50 things, so keep an eye out for them inside this book. They know loads of cool facts and have some great tips for exploring outdoors!

To find out your explorer type, try our quiz on page 12.

RAE
Age: 11¾
Likes: Photography, tennis and animals
Dislikes: Singing
Favourite activity: Bring up a butterfly
Explorer type: Animal lover

MIA
Age: 11
Likes: Growing her own vegetables and painting
Dislikes: Ketchup
Favourite activity: Plant it, grow it, eat it
Explorer type: Creative and crafty

Don't mind my little brother. He can be SO annoying. But he's ok really . . . Now, say 'CHEESE'!

Come on, it's time to get going. Adventure, here we come!

Using this book

So, now you've met the team, let's talk about how to get started on your 50 things.
Easy, right? Just get outside and have fun!
But don't forget to take this handbook – it's got all the tips you need for an amazing adventure, plus loads of other stuff to do!

Where to start?

You can start at the beginning, or do the activities in any order you like! And if you can't find what you're looking for, just turn to the index on page 94.

When you've completed an activity, sign your name and date at the bottom of the page – or stick a 50 things sticker over the circle. Stickers are available at participating National Trust properties.

Stick your sticker here / Stick your sticker here / Stick your sticker here / Stick your sticker here / Stick your sticker here

Date

_____

Signature

_____

Scrapbook

There's notepaper at the back of this book, along with space to stick in your photos. That means you can use this as a proper explorer's journal and fill it with notes, drawings, doodles, memories and more!

Fun and games

When you're in the car or relaxing at the end of a busy day, why not check out the quiz and puzzles in the activities section, starting on page 78?

> I LOVE taking photos – so my notebook's full of all the pictures I've taken!

There's also a 50 things website and app, where you can upload pictures, tick off your adventures and find events and places near you. When you finish all 50 things, you can go online to claim your secret reward!

What sort of explorer are you?

You're about to start a big adventure. And like all great explorers, you'll discover new places, encounter wild beasts and travel great distances (well, you'll go on a few long walks). But have you ever wondered what sort of explorer you are? Take this fun quiz and you'll soon find out.

Stay in with a book.

Reading the map at the front.

It's a rainy day. What do you do?

Grab your wellies – it's great puddle weather.

They're great for my art project.

START HERE

You go for a walk with your family. Where are you in the group?

At the back, looking for paw prints – there's a badger sett near here!

You find some feathers on the ground. What do you think?

You look around for a nest. What bird could it belong to?

What's at the top of your rucksack?

Compass →

Sketchpad →

GADGET WHIZZ

You never go out without your gadgets and you've got the perfect app for everything. You're great to have on a trip and always have the facts at your fingertips – but don't be afraid to jump in and get messy from time to time.

CREATIVE AND CRAFTY

You love drawing in your sketchbook, making wild art and gathering materials for your scrapbook – and you're always full of fantastic ideas! But that doesn't mean you can't be adventurous at the same time!

Start looking for the perfect shell. →

What's the first thing you do when you get to the beach?

Take your shoes off and jump right in! →

ACTIVE EXPLORER

You're always full of energy and you're the first to try out any new activity – whether it's climbing a tree or rolling down a hill. Don't forget to notice the little details in nature while you're having all that fun!

Let's build a raft! →

You come to a stream on your walk. What's your first thought?

Let's look for frogspawn! →

ANIMAL LOVER

You just love animals, and could watch them for hours! Your quiet, gentle nature means you're good at seeing nature in the wild, but don't forget it's fun to be really LOUD and SILLY sometimes!

13

Get ready

This handbook's all about YOU – it's your place to write ideas, draw what you see and stick in leaves, tickets, photos, or anything else! Now it's time to start writing in the book!

First, fill in this passport with all your explorer details. Find an old photo to stick in or, if you're feeling creative, you could draw a self-portrait instead!

EXPLORER PASSPORT

PHOTOGRAPH OR PICTURE

NAME

....

DATE OF BIRTH

....

HEIGHT

....

EYE COLOUR

....

Explorer's checklist

All explorers need a proper kitbag, too, so here are a few ideas for when you're packing. You won't need all these things at once, but the essentials are handy whatever adventure you're having!

The essentials:

- [ ] Walking shoes or trainers
- [ ] Water bottle
- [ ] Warm clothes
- [ ] Waterproof

And the rest:

- [ ] Notebook
- [ ] Pencil
- [ ] Suncream
- [ ] Map
- [ ] Compass
- [ ] Binoculars
- [ ] Net (for catching fish or bugs)
- [ ] Bucket
- [ ] String
- [ ] Torch
- [ ] Swimming clothes and towel
- [ ] Camera

Top tip!

Remember to think about the weather, and what activity you're planning. It will be a wet drive home if you forget to pack a towel for your sea-swimming trip!

Mapping

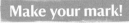

Having a map can be useful when you're an explorer. After all, you always need to find your way around. So here's a map of your very own!

Draw on it, write on it, and use it as a record of all your adventures. We even have a few ideas to get you started . . .

Make your mark!

- Draw a house or make a big dot to show where you live.
- As you go, mark the places where you've done your 50 things.
- Add more waves.
- Doodle dophins, whales and boats in the sea.
- If you go on a road trip, draw in the route you took.

Who knows where you might go to do your 50 things. But with this map you can keep track of everywhere you've been!

Scotland

Northern
Ireland

Republic of
Ireland

England

Wales

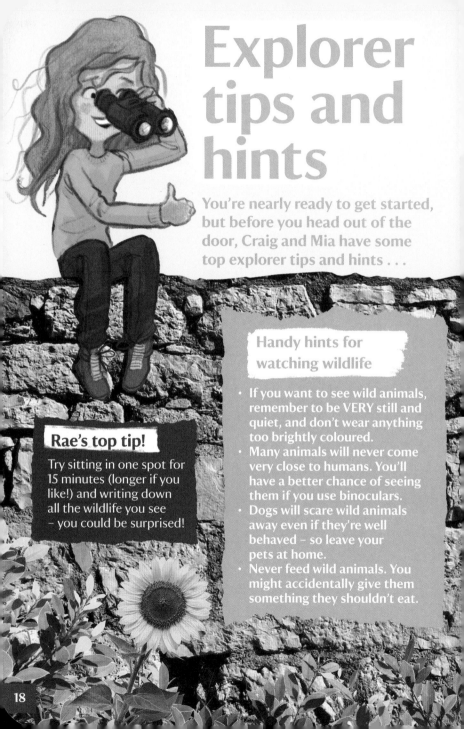

Explorer tips and hints

You're nearly ready to get started, but before you head out of the door, Craig and Mia have some top explorer tips and hints . . .

Handy hints for watching wildlife

- If you want to see wild animals, remember to be VERY still and quiet, and don't wear anything too brightly coloured.
- Many animals will never come very close to humans. You'll have a better chance of seeing them if you use binoculars.
- Dogs will scare wild animals away even if they're well behaved – so leave your pets at home.
- Never feed wild animals. You might accidentally give them something they shouldn't eat.

Rae's top tip!

Try sitting in one spot for 15 minutes (longer if you like!) and writing down all the wildlife you see – you could be surprised!

Make sure you stay safe and look after wildlife.
If in doubt, follow these simple rules!

The Countryside Code

1. Stay safe – plan your trip ahead.
2. Leave gates as you find them and follow local signs.
3. Always take your litter home.
4. Stay on the path – don't walk through crops.
5. Don't go near farm animals or machinery.
6. Don't climb over walls or hedges – use a gate or stile.
7. If your family has a dog, keep it under control.
8. Don't disturb other people.

Craig's top tip!

Get your friends to join
in too! See who can make
the biggest mud pie, fly
their kite the longest or
catch the biggest crab!

ADVENTURER

These 10 activities should be at the top of everyone's list! They're sure to give you a taste for ADVENTURE!

Top tip!
Don't forget to take lots of photos as you go. You can stick them in this book to remember your adventures!

1 Climb a tree

Do you know what type of tree you climbed?
See if its leaves match any of these:

✓ BIRCH

☐ SYCAMORE

☐ OAK

Or, why not draw your leaf here?

Stick your sticker here | Stick your sticker here | Stick your sticker here | Stick your sticker here | Stick your sticker here

Date
11/8/17

Signature
Emily + Max

Once you've climbed a tree, fill in the date to show you've completed this activity! Or you could stick in a 50 things sticker, from a National Trust property.

Remember that trees can be slippery if it's rained recently – it's a good idea to check before you climb.

21

2 Roll down a really big hill

It's the fun way to get to the bottom!

3 Camp out in the wild

Why sleep in a boring bed when you can sleep outside under the stars?

Date

_____

Signature

_____

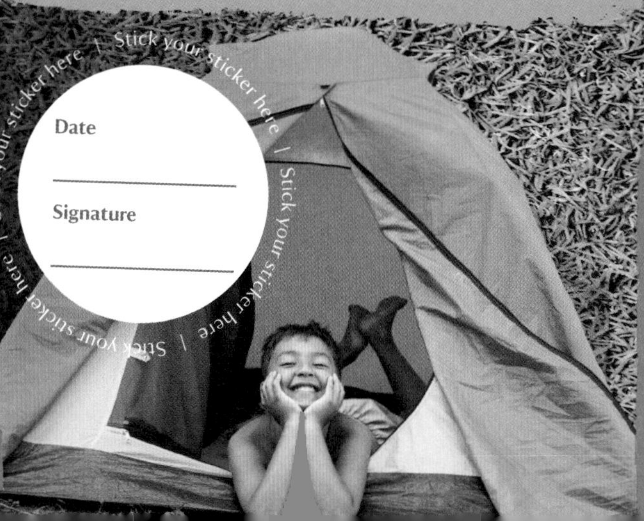

What nature sounds did you hear?

Did they sound like any of these animals?

What noise did you make rolling down the hill? Draw what you looked like when you got to the bottom here!

Check there are no steep drops or anything in the way (especially if it's brown and smelly) and off you go!

Stick your sticker here | Stick your sticker here | Stick your sticker here | Stick your sticker here | Stick your sticker here |

Date

_____

Signature

_____

☐ OWL

☐ FOX

☐ DEER

☐ HEDGEHOG

☐ OGRE

?

☐ YOUR FRIEND SNORING!

Did you know?

Being in a tent might mean you hear the dawn chorus, when songbirds sing at the start of a new day.

23

4 Build a den

Branches, twigs and leaves make surprisingly cosy dens.

5 Skim a stone

Can you do four bounces?

What type of skim did you do?

The Kamikaze

The Stealth

The Bouncer

Stick your favourite den photo in here! ←

Stick your sticker here | Stick your sticker here | Stick your sticker here | Stick your sticker here | Stick your sticker here

Date

_____

Signature

_____

Top tip!

Can't get your den to stand up? If you make a wigwam against a tree, it should stay up more easily.

Did you know?

As your old den rots, it will be eaten by fungi, insects and other creepy crawlies – all of which love rotting wood.

Top tip!

The best place to skim a stone is somewhere with flat water where there's a safe place to stand.

Stick your sticker here | Stick your sticker here | Stick your sticker here | Stick your sticker here

Date

_____

Signature

_____

Did you know?

Slate makes the best stones for skimming, and the smoother, rounder and flatter the better! Get low to the ground and throw your stone hard so it spins across the top of the water.

25

Run around in the rain

Time to make a splash!

After you're done splashing in the puddles, make a footprint on a piece of paper. Wait for it to dry, then cut it out and stick it in here!

Stick your sticker here | Stick your sticker here | Stick your sticker here | Stick your sticker here

Date
_____

Signature
_____

Fly a kite

Windy days are perfect for flying a kite.

Create your own kite design in the space below.

For your kite to really fly, it needs a nice clear sky, windy weather and a large open space – look out for trees, houses and pylons!

Stick your sticker here | Stick your sticker here | Stick your sticker here | Stick your sticker here

Date

_____

Signature

_____

8 Catch a fish with a net

You have to be quick to catch a fish!

What kind of fish did you see?
Do they match any of these?

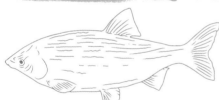
☐ ROACH

☐ DAB

☐ STICKLEBACK

☐ BUTTERFISH

Check out the 50 things app to find a place near you to catch a fish with a net!

Tell us more about the fish you caught . . .

What's your favourite fish?

....

How big is it?

....

What's its favourite food?

....

What's the best thing about it?

....

Can you draw your favourite fish here?

Stick your sticker here | Stick your sticker here | Stick your sticker here | Stick your sticker here | Stick your sticker here

Date

_____

Signature

_____

29

Eat an apple straight from a tree

9

I love apples!

Can you stick the pips from the apple you picked onto the page? Maybe you can feed the caterpillar . . .

Stick your sticker here | Stick your sticker here | Stick your sticker here | Stick your sticker here | Stick your sticker here

Date

_____

Signature

_____

Did you know?

There are more than 700 different types of apples in the UK. What's the name of the one you picked?

Bonkers for conkers!
How to get the best conker and beat your friends.

To choose a killer conker, put your conkers in a bucket of water; those that sink to the bottom are winners and those that float are losers.

Stick your sticker here | Stick your sticker here | Stick your sticker here | Stick your sticker here | Stick your sticker here

Date

_____

Signature

_____

Paint your conker and upload a photo to the website or app.

10
Play conkers

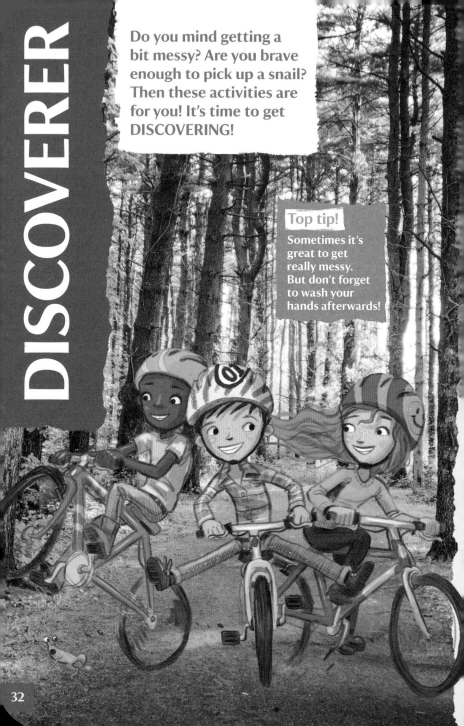

DISCOVERER

Do you mind getting a bit messy? Are you brave enough to pick up a snail? Then these activities are for you! It's time to get DISCOVERING!

Top tip!

Sometimes it's great to get really messy. But don't forget to wash your hands afterwards!

11 Go on a really long bike ride

The speedy way to explore the great outdoors!

Date
_____

Signature
_____

Stick your sticker here / Stick your sticker here / Stick your sticker here / Stick your sticker here / Stick your sticker here

Top places to cycle

1. Clumber Park, Nottinghamshire
2. Lanhydrock, Cornwall
3. Castle Ward, County Down
4. Wray Castle, Cumbria
5. Saltram, Devon
6. Wicken Fen NNR, Cambridgeshire

Show us how muddy you got!

Cycle over a piece of paper then stick it in here to show your tyre mark!

12 Make a trail with sticks

Use sticks as arrows and mark a path through the woods.

Why not capture some shots on the way around and upload them to the 50 things app?

Top tip!

Turn it into a treasure hunt by bringing something to hide at the end.

Stick your sticker here | Stick your sticker here | Stick your sticker here | Stick your sticker here |

Date

_____

Signature

_____

13 Make a mud pie

Recipe: Mud. More mud.

Stick your sticker here | Stick your sticker here | Stick your sticker here | Stick your sticker here | Stick your sticker here

Date

_____

Signature

_____

What sort of mud pie are you going to make? Why not draw it on this plate?

Top tip!

Every good pie needs some decorations. Stones, sticks, shells and leaves all make great mud pie toppings.

Dam a stream

It won't be long before
the stream's a pond!

How high is your dam?

Once you've managed to make
your pond, use the ruler on page
74 to see how high your dam is.

Stick your sticker here | Stick your sticker here | Stick your sticker here | Stick your sticker here | Stick your sticker here |

Date

_____

Signature

_____

Top tip!

Use larger rocks or twigs
near the middle of the
dam to make it as strong
as possible. Then fill in
the gaps with smaller
ones to make your dam
watertight.

Play in the snow

15

Keep your fingers cosy and your feet toasty.

Snowy ideas!
Have you done any of the list below?

- ☐ Make a snowman
- ☐ Build an igloo
- ☐ Create a snow angel
- ☐ Throw snowballs

Stick your sticker here | Stick your sticker here | Stick your sticker here | Stick your sticker here | Stick your sticker here | Stick your sticker here

Date

_____

Signature

_____

Did you know?

Snow is made from lots of tiny ice crystals, known as snowflakes. No two flakes are exactly the same.

Make a daisy chain

16

Perfect for summer days!

Stick your daisy chain here.

Set up a snail race

17

On your marks, get set, go . . . slowly.

Give the snails some racing colours!

Colour in the snails below to create your racing colours.

Date

_____

Signature

_____

Stick your sticker here | Stick your sticker here | Stick your sticker here | Stick your sticker here | Stick your sticker here

Take a photo of yourself wearing your daisy chain and upload it to the website or app.

50
11¾

Did you know?

Daisies don't really mind being picked, as it makes them grow more flowers!

Top tip!

Try to find daisies with long thick stems to make your chain. They will be easier to make holes in and less likely to break apart.

Did you know?

If you keep your snail cool and moist it will have the best chance of winning. Don't forget to put your snails back where you found them once they've finished racing.

Date

_____

Signature

_____

Stick your sticker here | Stick your sticker here | Stick your sticker here | Stick your sticker here | Stick your sticker here

Top tip!

Use tasty looking leaves to tempt your snail to move faster towards the finish line.

18 Create some wild art

Use leaves, sticks, pine cones or anything you like to create a work of art!

Exhibit your art in this frame!

Title of masterpiece:

50
11¾

Why not capture your wild art masterpiece and upload it to the 50 things app?

Stick your sticker here | Stick your sticker here | Stick your sticker here | Stick your sticker here | Stick your sticker here |

Date

_____

Signature

_____

Play pooh sticks 19

The best bridges for pooh sticks are traffic-free.

Who came first?

1st:

2nd:

3rd:

Top tip!

Decorate your stick by tying a leaf or some grass to it. You'll know exactly which one is yours when it comes out the other side of the bridge.

Stick your sticker here | Stick your sticker here | Stick your sticker here | Stick your sticker here | Stick your sticker here

Date

Signature

20 Jump over waves

Big, small, blue or green, all waves are great to jump over!

Try these jumps out!

Stick your sticker here | Stick your sticker here | Stick your sticker here | Stick your sticker here | Stick your sticker here

Date

Signature

THE SUPERMAN

THE GIANT LEAP

THE NINJA

Pick a spot where you know how deep the water is so you don't jump in where it's too deep!

41

RANGER

Are you ready to explore a bit further afield? Then grab your kitbag and get out there RANGER!

Top tip!

For ideas about where to go, just visit the 50 things website or app: 50things.org.uk

Pick blackberries growing in the wild

21

They're not just tasty treats, they make great drawing tools too!

Colour in the blackberry.
Blackberry juice makes the best paint . . .

Did you know?
The blackberry furthest along the branch, away from the centre of the blackberry bush, is the tastiest!

Stick your sticker here | Stick your sticker here | Stick your sticker here | Stick your sticker here | Stick your sticker here

Date

_____

Signature

_____

22

Explore inside a tree

Some trees have hollows so big you can climb right inside!

Date 18/9/17

Signature Emily

Did you know?

Lots of insects, such as beetles, live inside hollow trees and eat the rotting wood. Look closely and you'll see their burrowing holes.

Can you do a bark rubbing?

Place a piece of paper on a tree, rub over it with crayons and see what happens. Then use this space to stick in your bark rubbing!

23

Visit a farm

One of the best places to make new furry friends.

Make this page look like a farm!

Collect as many things as you can, like straw, feathers, wool, or whatever you like, and stick them on the page.

Can you match the farm animals to the footprints?

GOOSE

CHICKEN

HORSE

PIG

COW

Stick your sticker here | Stick your sticker here | Stick your sticker here | Stick your sticker here | Stick your sticker here

Date
_____

Signature
_____

After your farm visit, it's best to wash your hands clean of germs before eating and drinking.

45

Go on a walk
24 barefoot

You'll never want to put your shoes back on when you feel the tickly grass between your toes . . .

Stand here and draw around your toes!

Date

_____

Signature

_____

Keep your eyes peeled for glass or other things that might poke you.

25
Make a grass trumpet

Blow into a blade of grass and start up the band!

Stick your grass trumpet here.

Date

_____

Signature

_____

Stick here

How to make the best trumpet:

1. Pick your perfect piece of grass. Look for a long straight piece that's thick and dry.
2. Put your thumbs together, and hold the blade of grass between them, gripping the grass with the top and bottom of your thumbs.
3. Take the biggest breath you can and blow in-between your thumbs. As the air flows over the grass, you should hear a whistling sound.
4. If you don't hear anything, move the blade of grass a little and try again.

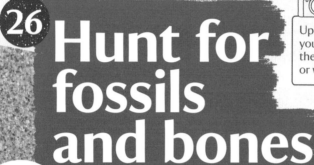

Hunt for fossils and bones

Upload a photo of your findings to the 50 things app or website.

27

GO stargazing

Stick your sticker here | Stick your sticker here | Stick your sticker here | Stick your sticker here | Stick your sticker here

Top tip!

Stargazing is best done before the moon is full, so it might be worth looking at the next new moon dates before you plan your stargazing evening.

Date

_____

Signature

_____

Can you join up the stars to create the constellations

See if you can spot them in the night sky.

Make sure you know the Fossil Code:

1. Stay away from cliffs and cliff edges.
2. Always go collecting when the tide is going out.
3. Be aware of weather conditions.
4. You can collect things which have been naturally unearthed or washed up.
5. Take a grown-up with you.

Stick your sticker here | Stick your sticker here | Stick your sticker here | Stick your sticker here | Stick your sticker here

Date

_____

Signature

_____

CASSIOPEIA

ORION

THE PLOUGH

Don't forget Orion's sword!

Can you spot the North Star?

Once you've found the plough, follow the two stars at the front of it upwards and you will find the North Star. This star was used by navigators to sail round the world as it meant they knew which way was north.

Keep an eye out for drops and edges!

Date

_____

Signature

_____

Stick your sticker here | Stick your sticker here | Stick your sticker here | Stick your sticker here | Stick your sticker here

28
Climb a huge hill

Go to the top and touch the sky!

Stick your sticker here | Stick your sticker here | Stick your sticker here | Stick your sticker here | Stick your sticker here

Date

_____

Signature

_____

29
Explore a cave

Don't forget your torch – you're going to need it!

Make a noise and listen for its echo. What did it sound like?

Top tip!
Bring an adult with you and follow good caving practice. Even experts never enter a cave alone!

Hold a scary beast

30

It might be scary at the time but think how brave you'll feel after!

What scary beast were you brave enough to hold?
Can you draw a picture of it?

There are loads of amazing scary beasts out there, like slimy slugs and big beetles. Avoid wasps, bees and brown furry caterpillars as they might bite or sting.

Stick your sticker here | Stick your sticker here | Stick your sticker here | Stick your sticker here | Stick your sticker here |

Date
_____

Signature
_____

51

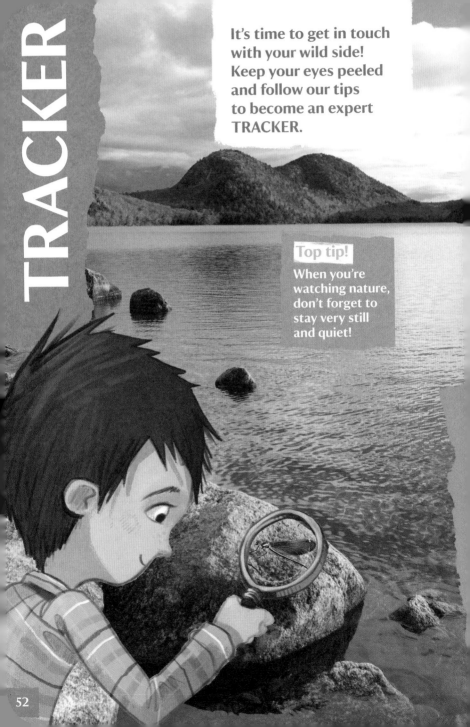

TRACKER

It's time to get in touch with your wild side! Keep your eyes peeled and follow our tips to become an expert TRACKER.

Top tip!

When you're watching nature, don't forget to stay very still and quiet!

31

Hunt for bugs

Stick your sticker here | Stick your sticker here | Stick your sticker here | Stick your sticker here | Stick your sticker here

Date

_____

Signature

_____

What's the creepiest crawly you can find?

Did you know?
There are more than 20,000 types of insect in the UK!

What creepy crawly did you catch? Can you draw it?

32

Find some frogspawn

Just wait until the tadpoles hatch!

Stick your sticker here | Stick your sticker here | Stick your sticker here | Stick your sticker here | Stick your sticker here

Date

_____

Signature

_____

Did you know?
Frogspawn looks like a thick jelly laid in clumps. Toadspawn looks similar but is laid in long chains.

53

34 Track wild animals

Top 3 tracking tips:

33 Catch a falling leaf

It's harder than you think!

Stick the leaves you caught here.

35 Discover what's in a pond

Pond water is full of life. Scoop some into a tub and check out what's living in it!

Stick your sticker here | Stick your sticker here | Stick your sticker here | Stick your sticker here | Stick your sticker here |

Date

_____

Signature

_____

Animals are easy to find if you follow their footprints, feathers, fur and poo . . .

1. Examine a footprint. How big is it? How many toes are there?

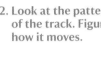

2. Look at the pattern of the track. Figure out how it moves.

3. Look for other signs. Does the animal have a tail?

What did you find?
Why not draw anything you spot below . . .

Top tip!
Scoop the net three times in a figure of eight to pick up the littlest creatures and empty the contents into a tub of water. If you don't spot anything at first, take a closer look.

Remember to return your new friends to their homes!

Make a home for a wild animal

36

It's not just dogs, cats, hamsters and fish that need homes!

Take a photo of your wild house and stick it here.

Stick your sticker here | Stick your sticker here | Stick your sticker here | Stick your sticker here | Stick your sticker here

Date

_____

Signature

_____

How to!

You could make an insect hotel, a hedgehog home or even a nesting box for birds. You can make an easy insect hotel just by placing sticks or plant stems in an empty plastic bottle.

37

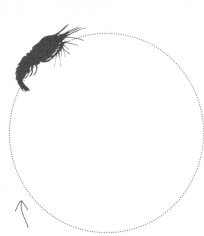

Check out the crazy creatures in a rock pool

What's the most amazing thing you can find?

Tell us more about the creature you saw . . .

What was it?

....

What colour was it?

....

How big was it?

....

Can you draw one of the creatures you saw in the circle above?

Stick your sticker here / Stick your sticker here / Stick your sticker here / Stick your sticker here / Stick your sticker here

Date

_____

Signature

_____

Did you know?

Starfish can push their stomachs out of their mouths so they can gobble up and digest anything that's too big to swallow.

Bring up a butterfly

Take a caterpillar home with you and you can watch it turn into a beautiful butterfly – then set it free and watch it fly away!

What you need to get started:

1. A caterpillar
2. A large plastic tub with small holes in the lid
3. Leaves from the plant where you found your caterpillar
4. Slightly damp soil to line the bottom of the tub
5. A twig or two to lean against the side of the tub

Keep a short diary!
Write down how your caterpillar changes at the end of each week.

Week 1

Week 2

Week 3

Week 4

Week 5

Week 6

Bring the butterflies to life!
Make them as colourful as you can and give them names.

Name:

Name:

Top tip!

Avoid hairy caterpillars as some can sting. Check out the 50 things website for more advice on how to choose and look after your caterpillar.

Stick your sticker here | Stick your sticker here | Stick your sticker here | Stick your sticker here | Stick your sticker here

Date
_____

Signature
_____

59

Catch a crab

Stick your sticker here | Stick your sticker here | Stick your sticker here

Stick your sticker here | Stick your sticker here

Date
_____

Signature
_____

Top tip!

Scraps of bacon and fish make really good crab bait.

Date
_____

Signature
_____

Stick your sticker here | Stick your sticker here | Stick your sticker here | Stick your sticker here | Stick your sticker here

Can you join up the dots and finish this crab?

See if you can draw in its feet and claws to help it reach the bait!

Why not try switching off your torch for 10 minutes. Can you see in the dark or hear any animals?

How to:

Tie a stone and bait to the end of some string so that it sinks properly. When you feel the string tugging, pull it up at a good pace – too quickly and the crab will fall off, too slowly and it will eat all the bait. Be very careful when you pick crabs up (they're not afraid to use those pincers) and don't forget to put them back in the water afterwards.

Top tip!

Plan your walk for a full moon so you can see where you're going!

Take a grown-up with you.

EXPLORER

Are you ready for a challenge? These adventurous activities are ones you won't forget in a hurry!
Let's go EXPLORING!

Top tip!

These aren't all things you'd try every day. Why not look up events or classes in your area? Visit the 50 things website to learn more.

Plant it, grow it, eat it

41

Just like you, fruit and vegetables need time to grow, but they're definitely worth the wait . . .

How's it growing?
Draw a picture and measure your plant's height to show how well it's been growing.

Week 1

....

Week 2

....

Week 3

....

50
11¾

Why not take shots of your plant as it grows and upload them to the 50 things app?

Stick your sticker here | Stick your sticker here | Stick your sticker here | Stick your sticker here | Stick your sticker here

Date

_____

Signature

_____

Top tip!
Old wellies and even jam jars make really great places to grow your plants. Just add soil!

Go swimming in the sea

42

Bounce over waves whilst practising your backstroke.

Can you mark around the map where you've been for a swim?

Build a raft

43

Take to the water in your homemade raft – but be prepared for it to sink!

How to:

1. First you need something to make your raft float. Look for empty barrels or collect used drinks bottles. Anything full of air will do.
2. Next, make the body of your raft – most rafts have a basic wooden frame.
3. Tie your floats together and fix them to the raft's body.
4. If your raft is big enough to carry you, don't forget to wear a life jacket!

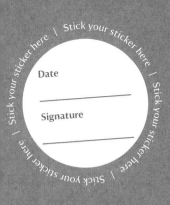

Date

_____

Signature

_____

Stick your sticker here | Stick your sticker here | Stick your sticker here | Stick your sticker here | Stick your sticker here

Top tip!

To stay safe, only swim on beaches with lifeguards, and always follow their signs and instructions.

The sea can be powerful, so make sure you have a grown-up with you and only swim where the water is calm.

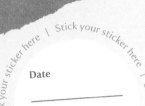

Date

_____

Signature

_____

Stick your sticker here | Stick your sticker here | Stick your sticker here | Stick your sticker here

Stick in a photo of your raft.

If you don't fancy getting wet, why not make a mini raft by tying some twigs together with long pieces of grass or straw? Stick in a leaf for a sail and set your raft on the water!

Top tip!

With a grown-up, launch your raft from a calm section of water.

65

44

Go bird watching

Be as quiet as a mouse and watch the birds at play.

Don't forget your binoculars!

What type of birds did you spot?

Do they match any of the drawings below?

☐ PIGEON

Look out for robins' red tummies →

☐ ROBIN

Or why not draw your bird here?
↓

☐ HERRING GULL

Stick your sticker here / Stick your sticker here / Stick your sticker here / Stick your sticker here / Stick your sticker here /

Date

_____

Signature

_____

Did you know?

Nearly 600 different types of bird have been seen in the UK!

45

Find your way with a map and compass

You'll never get lost if you can use these trusty tools.

Draw your own map of where you went and what you saw here.

Did you know?

This shape, called a compass rose, is often found on maps and compasses. The different points on the rose mark where North, East, South and West are.

Stick your sticker here / Stick your sticker here / Stick your sticker here / Stick your sticker here / Stick your sticker here / Stick your sticker here /

Date

_____

Signature

_____

46 Try rock climbing

Keep your eyes peeled for some big cracks and places to get a good grip.

Top tip!

Only climb in a safe, supervised setting and remember to ALWAYS wear a helmet when you are rock climbing.

This isn't the kind of thing you can do every day. Why not join a class at a climbing centre near you? Visit the 50 things website to find out more.

☐ The sky

☐ Big Ben

☐ A tree

☐ A car

Stick your sticker here / Stick your sticker here / Stick your sticker here / Stick your sticker here / Stick your sticker here /

Date

_____

Signature

_____

Did you know?

The youngest person to climb Mount Everest so far was only 13!

How high did you climb?

Cook on a campfire

There's no kitchen in the great outdoors but you don't have to miss dinner!

Draw your very own campfire meal in the pan!

50
11¾

Why not take a shot of your meal and upload it to the 50 things app?

Top tip!

Jacket potatoes are great camping food. Potatoes can easily be wrapped in foil and cooked in a fire. Serve them up with some baked beans!

Stick your sticker here | Stick your sticker here | Stick your sticker here | Stick your sticker here | Stick your sticker here | Stick your sticker here |

Date
_____

Signature
_____

Learn to ride a horse

Soon you'll be riding like a proper jockey!

Why not design your own racing colours?

What was your horse called?

Name:

50
11¾

Check out the 50 things app to see if there are any riding classes near you.

Stick your sticker here / Stick your sticker here / Stick your sticker here / Stick your sticker here / Stick your sticker here

Date

Signature

49

Find a geocache

For all those who love a treasure hunt outdoors!

What did you find in your geocache?

What did you put in it for others to come and find?

Stick your sticker here | Stick your sticker here | Stick your sticker here | Stick your sticker here | Stick your sticker here | Stick your sticker here

Date

_____

Signature

_____

Did you know!

The first recorded geocache was in Oregon, USA in 2000.

This isn't the kind of thing you can do every day so why not look up an outdoor activity centre? Visit the 50 things website to find out more.

Canoe down a river

50

See the world from a duck's point of view.

☐ DRAGONFLY

☐ OTTER

☐ SWAN

What did you see by the riverside?

Stick your sticker here / Stick your sticker here / Stick your sticker here / Stick your sticker here / Stick your sticker here

Date
_____

Signature
_____

☐ KINGFISHER

You did it!

Well done! You completed all 50 things! So how was it? We hope you had a fantastic adventure!

Now that you're done, don't let those memories fade. Use the next few pages to record all your very best bits. Then why not have a go at some of our puzzles?

50
11¾

Don't forget you can share your adventures online or using the 50 things app!

Wondering why there's a ruler here? Just turn the page to find out . . .

19
18
17
16
15
14
13
12
11
10
9
8
7
6
5
4
3
2
1 cm

Ruler

Some of the activities in this book need a ruler. But if you haven't got one with you, just cut along the dotted line and use the ruler on this page!

You might be surprised at how small – or BIG! – some animals are. Why not note down any measurements you take on this page?

Top fact!

Did you know that the pygmy shrew is the smallest mammal in the UK, at only 7cm long?

pygmy shrew – 7cm

millipede – 6cm

acorn – 3cm

bee – 1cm

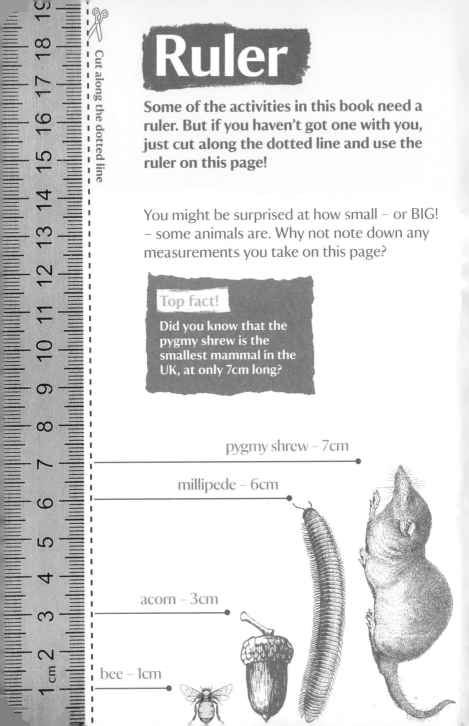

My favourites

What did you think of the activities? Was there one that made you mucky? Or one you found a bit scary?

Fill in this table with the messiest, noisiest and silliest things you've tried!

	Which activity	Why I liked it
Messiest		
Noisiest		
Scariest		
Most beautiful		
Most exciting		
Most difficult		
Best with friends		
Best with animals		
Best at night		
Best in summer		
Best in winter		

Add some more ideas here!

The winner is . . .

So what was your absolute FAVOURITE activity?
Well, we think it deserves a prize for being
so great, don't you?

**Fill in this page
to make it
all about your
personal No.1!**

1st

Doodle in
loads more
decoration.

Colour the
rosette in your
favourite colour.

Complete the
details on the
trophy.

No.1 Activity:

....

Date awarded:

....

Completed by (name):

....

Other things to try

Can you think of 10 more things you want to do before you're 11¾? They could be anything from surfing to archery. List them here:

1 ....

2 ....

3 ....

4 ....

5 ....

6 ....

7 ....

8 ....

9 ....

10 ....

Doodle time

Whether you're on a long car journey, lounging on the beach, or chilling in the park, these activities are just what you need to keep you busy. So grab a pen or pencil and get to it!

Colour in Rae's umbrella.

Add more splashes to this puddle.

Fill the branches with birds or leaves.

You could even draw a rainbow in the sky!

Who do you think lives in this hollow?

Complete the flowers!

Fill in the gaps!

Dot to dot

Something's been left behind in the grass. But what is it?

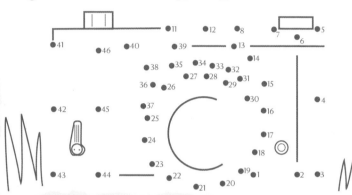

Picture perfect

Can you copy this picture of Craig? It's not as hard as it sounds! Just use the grid and copy one square at a time.

Fill in the missing words to make up your own story. You can use whatever words and names you want!

THE NEWS

FAMOUS EXPLORER MAKES GREAT DISCOVERY!

Today, world-famous explorer

_____ has made a

fantastic discovery! While trekking

across _____,

the explorer's team saw a strange

_____ and decided to

follow it. This led them to an

enormous _____.

Speaking about their find,

the expedition leader _____

said, "I've been exploring the great

outdoors since I was _____ years old,

PHOTOGRAPH OR PICTURE

and I never thought I'd see anything like this _____.

It's definitely the _____ I've ever seen!

It's been a _____ expedition, but none of it would have

been possible without the help of my _____ and _____."

This discovery will make _____ one of the most famous

_____ in the _____!

Puzzles

Once you've finished the puzzles, you can check the answers on page 87!

Wordsearch

Can you find 15 animals hidden in the grid? They could be vertical, horizontal, diagonal or backwards!

Y	D	R	I	B	K	C	A	L	B
L	Z	F	S	R	A	S	M	A	A
F	T	I	B	B	A	R	D	M	T
R	D	S	W	P	J	G	C	O	P
E	O	H	O	F	E	Y	I	U	N
T	L	E	R	R	I	U	Q	S	H
T	P	Y	M	O	B	R	X	E	B
U	H	E	D	G	E	H	O	G	D
B	I	W	S	E	G	K	N	T	F
O	N	R	D	P	E	E	H	S	Z

Badger
Bat
Blackbird
Butterfly
Crab
Deer
Dolphin
Fish
Frog
Hedgehog
Mouse
Rabbit
Sheep
Squirrel
Worm

Sudoku

Finish this grid so that each row, column and block of four squares contains a kite, a flower, a fish and a star.

Crossword

Solve the clues to fill in the missing nature words!

Across
1. Squirrels gather these (6)
2. A baby butterfly (11)
5. Birds make one in spring (4)
6. A bird with a red chest (5)

Down
1. The best time of year for playing conkers (6)
2. A rock pool creature with big pincers (4)
3. A cluster of frogs' eggs (9)
4. Where you sleep when you go camping (4)

Word scramble

Unscramble these words to find seven items you might pack in your kitbag. (For clues turn to page 15.)

tware _ _ _ _ _

remaca _ _ _ _ _ _

pma _ _ _

sampocs _ _ _ _ _ _ _

ten _ _ _

chort _ _ _ _ _

nsumarec _ _ _ _ _ _ _ _

Maze

Oh dear. It looks like Mia's got lost in this maze! Can you help her find her way out?

EXIT

Quick-fire quiz

You might be surprised to know how many of the 50 things have made it into the record books . . .

Test your knowledge or try these questions on your friends! The answers are on page 87!

1) How big is the largest kite ever?
- ☐ a) 40 metres across
- ☐ b) 5 metres across
- ☐ c) 100 metres across

2) What is the record number of skips skimming a stone on water?
- ☐ a) 12
- ☐ b) 88
- ☐ c) 204

3) The World Conkers Championship takes place every year. How many people took place in the largest championship ever?
- ☐ a) 395
- ☐ b) 5,000
- ☐ c) 42

4) When was the first compass invented?
- ☐ a) Around 1400 AD
- ☐ b) Around 100 AD
- ☐ c) Around 300 BC

5) What is the world record for miles cycled in one year?
- ☐ a) 75,065 miles (three times around the world)
- ☐ b) 904 miles
- ☐ c) 150,256 miles

6) What is the greatest height ever rock-climbed in one day?
- ☐ a) 507 metres
- ☐ b) 100 metres
- ☐ c) 8,880 metres

7) The snail racing championships take place in Norfolk every year. What is the record time for a snail to complete the 33cm course?
- ☐ a) 23 seconds
- ☐ b) 2 minutes
- ☐ c) 20 minutes

8) How old is the oldest known tree in the UK?
- ☐ a) 400 years old
- ☐ b) 150 years old
- ☐ c) At least 4,000 years old

9) What is the longest solo journey made in a canoe?
- ☐ a) 150,057 miles
- ☐ b) 90 miles
- ☐ c) 2,010 miles

10) How large is the biggest species of crab in the world?
- ☐ a) 3.8 metres
- ☐ b) 20 centimetres
- ☐ c) 9.1 metres

Answers

So how did you do?
Check your answers here!

Wordsearch

Y	D	R	I	B	K	C	A	L	B
L	Z	F	S	R	A	S	M	A	A
F	T	I	B	B	A	R	O	M	T
R	D	S	W	P	J	G	C	O	P
E	O	H	O	F	E	Y	I	U	N
T	L	E	R	R	I	U	Q	S	H
T	P	Y	M	O	B	R	X	E	B
U	H	E	D	G	E	H	O	G	D
B	I	W	S	E	G	K	N	T	F
O	N	R	D	P	E	E	H	S	Z

Crossword

	¹A	C	O	R	N	S			³	
	U								F	
²C	A	T	E	R	P	I	L	L	A	R
R	U								O	
A	U		⁴						G	
B	⁵M	N	E	S	T				S	
			E						P	
			N						A	
			T						W	
						⁶R	O	B	I	N

Sudoku

Word scramble

1. Water, 2. Camera,
3. Map, 4. Compass,
5. Net, 6. Torch,
7. Suncream

Maze

Quiz

1 (a); 2 (b); 3 (a); 4 (c);
5 (a); 6 (c); 7 (b); 8 (c);
9 (c); 10 (a)

87

Picture gallery

Stick your photos here or doodle in the frames.

Notepaper

Use these pages to jot things down while you're out and about!

A

50 + 10 + 50 + 20 + 30 + 50
+ 30 + 50 + 50 + 50

340

50 + 20 + 50 + 50 + 20
+ 10 + 40 + 50 + 30 + 20

340

Index

Acknowledgements

t = top, b = bottom, c = centre, l = left, r = right, f = far

Cover (c), p20 © Dudarev Mikhail/ Shutterstock.com; cover (b) © canadastock/Shutterstock.com; cover, p27, 42 (t), 74, 75, 77 © winnond/Shutterstock.com; p1 Stock photo © Kritchanut; p6 (b,r) © Andrew Burgess/Shutterstock.com; p6 (bl), 74 (fl) © Maryna S/Shutterstock.com; p6 (b), 48, 61 © Prapann/Shutterstock; p7 © Zepedrocoelho/Shutterstock.com; p8-9, 22-23, 51, 69 (b), 76-77 © Jiraphoto/Shutterstock.com; p10 © suns07butterfly/Shutterstock.com; p11 © rzarek/Shutterstock. com; p12 © JGade/Shutterstock.com; p13 (cr) © Tribalium/Shutterstock.com; p13 (tl) © pixelprohd/ Shutterstock.com; p 13 (l), 58 Stock photo © istockpLisa Thornberg; p15 (r) © jukurae/Shutterstock. com; p15 (bl) © Rost9/Shutterstock.com; p15 (bc) © Bildagentur Zoonar GmbH/Shutterstock. com; p15 (tr) © Marynka/Shutterstock.com; p16 (tr) © bsd/Shutterstock.com; p16 (b), 24 (b) © elegeyda/Shutterstock.com; p17 (c) © Jamie Farrant/Shutterstock.com; p17 (b) © Elena Kazanskaya/ Shutterstock.com; p18-19 (c) © chrupka/Shutterstock.com; p18-19 (b) Ian 2010/Shutterstock.com; p18-19 (bl) © napas chalermchai/Shutterstock.com; p21 © Miro art studio/Shutterstock.com; p22 (bl) © Kokhanchikov/ Shutterstock.com; p23 (c), 33 (c), 57 (c, tr) © thumbelina/Shutterstock. com; p23 (fl) © Vasilyeva Larisa/ Shutterstock.com; p23 (l) © La puma/ Shutterstock.com; p 23 (bl) © Dean Murray/ Shutterstock.com; p23 (r) © moopsi/ Shutterstock.com; p 23 (fr) © Ilya Zonov/ Shutterstock.com; p24 (tl) © gdvcom/ Shutterstock.com; p24 (tl) © bawan/Shutterstock.com; p24, 25 © NRT/Shutterstock.com; p25 (tl) © Natalia Sheinkin/Shutterstock.com; p26 © almgren/ Shutterstock.com; p27 (t, b) © Annette Shaff/Shutterstock.com; p28-29, 61, 65 (l) © Anthonycz/ Shutterstock.com; p28 (bl) © National Trust/Rob Salter; p29 © Tribalium/Shutterstock.com; p30 (t), 58 (cr) © Vector/Shutterstock.com; p30 (c) © TomZa/Shutterstock.com; p30 (b) © raysay/ Shutterstock.com; p31 (tr) © MARKBZ/Shutterstock.com; p32 © Karen Grigoryan/Shutterstock. com; p33 (c) © greenland/Shutterstock.com; p33 (r) © Jason Winter/Shutterstock.com; p 34 (l), 36, 41 (tr), 69 (b) © graphixmania/Shutterstock.com; p34, 35 © Strejman/Shutterstock.com; p 34, 35 © diogoppr/Shutterstock.com; p 35 (b) © Andrey_Kuzmin/Shutterstock.com; p36 © Festa/ Shutterstock.com; p37 © Max Topchii/Shutterstock.com; p38, 39 (c) © chrisbrignell/Shutterstock. com; p39 (b) © pio3/Shutterstock.com; p40 © National Trust Images; p41 (br) © Leremy/ Shutterstock.com; p42 © ollirg/Shutterstock.com; p43 (c, tr) © Anna Kucherova/Shutterstock.com; p43 © Linda Vostrovska/Shutterstock.com; p44 © Conny Sjostrom/Shutterstock.com; p45 (t, c), 66 (c), 70 (c, r), 74 (f4) © Nouwens/Shutterstock.com; p45 (bl), 55 (t) © Helga Chirk/Shutterstock.com; p46 (br) © TravnikovStudio/Shutterstock.com; p47 (c) © julie deshaies/Shutterstock.com; p47 (b) © Lina Valunaite/Shutterstock.com; p48 (tr) © MIGUEL GARCIA SAAVEDRA/Shutterstock.com; p48 (cr) © IhorZigor/Shutterstock.com; p49 © Janos Levente/Shutterstock.com; p50 © IR Stone/ Shutterstock.com; p51 (l) © Vitalii Hulai/Shutterstock.com; p51 (bl) © Eric Isselee/Shutterstock. com; p52 © JaysonPhotography/Shutterstock.com; p52 (b), 53 (t) © Dmitriy Kurnyavko/ Shutterstock.com; p53 (b) © BMJ/Shutterstock.com; p54 © Fotofermer/Shutterstock.com; p54 (br) © Chros/Shutterstock.com; p55 (br) © sarininka/Shutterstock.com; p56 © THPStock/Shutterstock. com; p57 Stock photo © Peter Mukherjee; p59 Stock photo © Stepan_Bormotov; p60 © A7880S/ Shutterstock.com; p61 © Nuttapong/Shutterstock.com; p62 © Helen Hotson/Shutterstock. com; p64 (t) © s_oleg/Shutterstock.com; p64 (br) © Ramona Heim/Shutterstock.com; p65 (b) Stock photo © dghagi; p66 (l) © chronicler/Shutterstock.com; p66 (r) © aggressor/Shutterstock. com; p66 (bl) © Fotonium/Shutterstock.com; p67 (cr) © Visual Idiot/Shutterstock.com; p67 (tr) © sergign/Shutterstock.com; p69 (bc) © AkeSak/Shutterstock.com; p70 (tr) © Rashad Ashurov/ Shutterstock.com; p71 © National Trust Images/John Millar; p72 (t) © marekuliasz/Shutterstock. com; p72 (l) © Dn Br/Shutterstock.com; p72 (c) © chronicler/Shutterstock.com; p72 (b) © Wolf Drawing/Shutterstock.com; p72 (r) © shooarts/Shutterstock.com; p74 (r) © Morphart Creation/ Shutterstock.com; p74 (l) © Liliya Shlapak/Shutterstock.com; p76 (t) © Alex Leo/Shutterstock.com; p76 (c) © mamanamsai/Shutterstock.com; p88-89 © Irina Vaneeva/Shutterstock.com; p90-91 © Sheryl C.S. Johnson/Shutterstock.com; p92-93 © rzarek/Shutterstock.com